Mythologies

Dragons

John Malam

QEB Publishing

Copyright © QEB Publishing, Inc. 2009

Published in the United States by
QEB Publishing, Inc.
3 Wrigley, Suite A
Irvine, CA 92618
www.qeb-publishing.com

Library of Congress Cataloging-in-Publication Data

Malam, John, 1957-
   Dragons / John Malam.
      p. cm. -- (QEB mythology)
   Includes index.
   ISBN 978-1-59566-982-7 (hardcover)
   1. Dragons--Juvenile literature. I. Title.
GR830.D7M35 2010
398.24'54--dc22
                    2008056082

Author John Malam
Editor Amanda Learmonth
Designer Lisa Peacock
Illustrator Vincent Follenn

Publisher Steve Evans
Creative Director Zeta Davies
Managing Editor Amanda Askew

Picture credits

(t=top, b=bottom, l=left, r=right, c=center, fc=front cover)
Alamy Images 5bl Pictures Colour Library, 9 The London Art
Archive, 13t INTERFOTO Pressebildagentur, 13b Leslie
Garland Picture Library, 17b Mary Evans Picture Library,
21 Pictor International/Image State, 27t Malcolm Park
Astronomy images
Corbis 11b Bettmann, 29 Lindsay Hebberd
Dreamstime 23
Getty Images Getty Images 4t The Image Bank/Chris Alan
Wilton, 4b Visuals Unlimited/Ken Lucas, 15t AFP/Stringer,
15c Lonely Planet Image/Jane Sweeney
Istockphoto 5bc Maris Zemgalietis
Mary Evans Picture Library 5tr, 5cr
Photolibrary 25 Robert Harding Travel
Shutterstock 5tc Martina Orlich, 5br Javarman,
20 Jean-Michel Olives
Topham Picturepoint 5tl Fortean, 7 The British Library

Words in **bold** are explained
in the glossary on page 30.

CONTENTS

The world of dragons

Stories have been told about dragons for thousands of years. Countries all over the world have myths about these fabulous creatures, and there are many tales that speak of the daring deeds of **dragon-slayers**.

Dragons are often described as the guardians of valuable treasure or captured princesses. They are among the most dangerous of all mythical creatures, and the hardest to defeat. All dragons have scaly skin. Many have fiery breath or poisonous, stinging tails. Some have wings, others don't. Some are short, others are long and have the twisting bodies of giant **serpents**.

⬆ *The dragon is one of the most fabulous creatures in mythology.*

⬇ *Dinosaur skeletons may have led people to believe in dragons.*

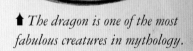

From dinosaur to dragon

Long ago, when ancient bones from dinosaurs were found in the ground, no one knew what creatures they had come from. These mysterious bones might have led people to make up stories about terrifying creatures, such as dragons.

Who's who among the dragons?

Dragons from European folklore

Cockatrice
A monster with a dragon's body and wings, and the head and legs of a cockerel.

European dragon
A fire-breathing, winged beast with scaly skin, long legs, and sharp claws.

Worm
A dragon with a huge, snake-like body.

Basilisk
Similar to the cockatrice, but with eight cockerel legs and a poisonous bite.

Dragons from folklore around the world

Chinese and Japanese dragon
A lizardlike beast without wings but with a horned head, scaly skin, and sharp claws.

Babylonian and ancient Middle Eastern dragon
A wingless beast with eagle's legs at the rear and cat's legs at the front.

Indian dragon
A monstrous serpent with three heads.

5

Dragons of Europe

Ever since the time of the ancient Greeks, 2,500 years ago, dragons have been part of European mythology.

The ancient Greeks thought of dragons as massive serpents that lived at the ends of the world where they guarded great treasures. The most famous was Ladon, a giant serpent with 100 heads and 200 fiery eyes. It guarded a tree of golden apples.

European dragons are often described as winged beasts with fiery breath.

Saints and dragons

In Christian mythology, St. George is a well-known dragon-slayer. He was not the only **saint** to defeat a dragon. St. Martha managed to tame Tarasque, a dragon that terrified the south of France.

During Roman times (about 2,000 years ago), the Romans spoke of dragons that lived in Ethiopia, East Africa. It was believed these monsters were snakelike creatures that breathed fire, had wings, were about 60 feet (18 meters) long and ate the flesh of elephants.

➡ *This page from a "bestiary" (a book about beasts from the Middle Ages) shows what dragons were thought to look like.*

Dragons at war

When Roman soldiers went into battle in the AD 300s, a dragon went with them. It was a **standard** (a type of flag), shaped as a dragon-headed serpent. In the AD 600s, a red dragon became a symbol of Wales, UK. Warriors carried dragon flags into battle. The greatest warriors were given the title "**pendragon**," meaning "dragon head," or leader.

At the start of the **Middle Ages** (from about AD 450), dragons were seen as evil creatures. Myths spoke of Christian saints whose duty was to slay dragons and defeat evil. Between the 1100s and 1400s, books known as "bestiaries" described dragons in great detail. People believed these monsters really existed.

Once upon a time: Beowulf and the dragon

DENMARK

This myth comes from…

In the kingdom of the Danes, the monster Grendel struck fear into the hearts of all men. Each night, Grendel came from the swamp, and no matter how hard they fought, the Danes were always defeated.

➤ *Beowulf was a dragon-slayer and hero of the Danes.*

In time, a warrior called Beowulf came to Denmark and killed Grendel. When the monster's mother wanted revenge, he killed her, too. Beowulf became a hero, and his fame spread far and wide.

Many years later, Beowulf fought a dragon that guarded buried treasure. Thieves disturbed the dragon in its **lair**, and it breathed fire across the land.

→ *A gold clasp from the Sutton Hoo treasure. It is decorated with red stones called garnets.*

The Sutton Hoo treasure

In 1939, gold and silver treasure was found inside a burial mound at Sutton Hoo, Suffolk, England. It is believed to have belonged to a king from the AD 600s. Like Beowulf, the king was buried inside an earthen mound. This was the custom at the time for some important people.

Beowulf took up his sword. He fought the dragon, but its scales were like armor and Beowulf's weapon was useless.

Another warrior came to Beowulf's help, and between them the dragon was killed. But there was a price to pay. Beowulf had been bitten by the dragon. As its deadly poison flowed through his veins, his life came to an end. The warrior was laid to rest with great treasure in a burial mound beside the sea.

Once upon a time:
The man who became a dragon

This myth comes from…

- SCANDINAVIA
- GERMANY

Greed is a terrible thing, and there are those who never learn this. Take a man called Fafnir, and his brothers Ottar and Regin.

Ottar was able to change himself into other beings. One day, he changed into an otter. The god Loki thought he was a real otter, and killed him. The brothers' father then demanded Loki pay for his crime. Loki did this, by giving him gold, but the gold was **cursed**, so bad luck would always follow it.

When they saw their father's gold, Fafnir and Regin were filled with greed. The brothers killed their father, but Fafnir stole the gold and ran far away. He changed into a terrifying dragon, and lay on the treasure to guard it.

⬇ *The greedy brothers killed their father and stole his gold.*

Regin wanted revenge, and he wanted the treasure. He went to Sigurd, a brave warrior, for help. Regin gave him a magic sword, which Sigurd used to slay Fafnir the dragon. Regin claimed the treasure, but the curse passed on to him. Regin was killed by Sigurd, who took the treasure for himself. Then the curse was again passed on, and he, too, was doomed to die.

➡ *Sigurd slayed Fafnir the dragon with his magic sword.*

◀ *A Viking "drakkar," or **dragonship**.*

Dragonships

The story of Fafnir the dragon was told by the **Vikings** of Scandinavia and northern Europe. Some of their **longships** had carvings of dragons' heads on their prows (fronts). The Vikings called these ships "drakkar," or dragonships.

Sigurd the dragon-slayer

After Sigurd killed Fafnir, he licked the blood from his fingers. This gave him the power to understand the language of birds. Two birds then told him that Regin planned to kill him.

Once upon a time:
The dragon that crash-landed

In the year 1421, a dragon was flying to Mount Pilatus, near Lucerne, Switzerland. It was one of the many dragons that lived in caves high on the mountain's snowy peak.

On its way home, the dragon crashed to the ground and startled a farmer who was out walking. When the farmer, whose name was Stempflin, saw the great beast flapping its wings and trying to take off, he fainted.

Stempflin had no idea how long he lay on the ground, but he awoke with a start. He looked for the dragon, but it was nowhere to be seen. Would anyone believe his story, or would they say he had fallen asleep and had a dream?

Helpful dragons

Unlike many dragons, the Mount Pilatus dragons are thought of as friendly and helpful. They are believed to heal the sick and rescue travelers lost in the mountains.

⬇ *The dragon crashed to the ground, startling Farmer Stempflin.*

⬆ *Mount Pilatus is believed to be the home of the friendly dragons.*

WHAT IS A DRAGON-STONE?

Red-colored stones are sometimes called "**dragon-stones**." They are thought to be hardened lumps of dragons' blood.

⬆ *Cinnabar is a red-colored stone, also known as a "dragon-stone."*

The confused farmer went over to where the dragon had crashed, and saw a pool of blood. It was the dragon's blood, and in the middle was a strange, red stone. Stempflin knew it to be a dragon-stone. He picked it up and took it home. From that day on it brought him good luck, as it had the power to cure any illness or injury.

Dragons of the Middle East

Some of the world's first dragon stories ever told come from the countries of the Middle East. These tales were told by ancient peoples known as Sumerians, Babylonians and Assyrians.

The stories go back about 5,000 years. They describe how the world began, and the struggle between the forces of good and evil. Dragons were thought of as evil monsters that people had to kill or make peace with.

Dragons in the Bible

Dragons are mentioned in the Christian Bible. They may come from stories that spread across the Middle East. For example, in the Bible there is a "red dragon with seven heads and ten horns." It stands for the Devil.

↓ *Anzu was a birdlike monster with a lion's head. It caused sandstorms when it flapped its wings.*

➡ *Dahak was a serpent monster with two snake heads and one human head.*

↑ A dragon picture on the Ishtar Gate, Babylon.

In ancient times, visitors to the city of Babylon, in modern-day Iraq, walked through a gateway in the city wall. The gateway, which was made about 575 BC, was decorated with pictures of dragons and other fierce creatures. Visitors could have no doubt that they were entering an important, powerful city.

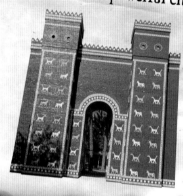

They came in many forms. Some were imagined as giant serpents, others as creatures made from the body parts of different animals. No matter what they looked like, all of them were powerful and terrifying beings.

↓ Musrussu was a giant serpent with the front feet of a cat, the back legs of a bird, and a tail with a poisonous sting.

↓ Tiamat was a huge sea snake with two forelegs, a giant tail, and horns on its head.

↓ Leviathan was a sea monster with seven heads and hundreds of eyes.

Once upon a time: How the world began

IRAQ

This myth comes from…

In the time before Heaven and Earth were created, only chaos existed. It was a time of nothingness, a time of confusion.

Then, from the nothingness, two creatures appeared. They were Tiamat, the mother of the salty sea, and Abzu, the father of freshwater rivers and lakes. From these beings the first gods were born. One of them was Enki.

As the gods grew, they quarreled. This upset their father Abzu who wished to kill them all. But Enki was cunning —he killed his father to save his own life.

← *The young gods argued and fought each other, which upset their father, Abzu.*

Tiamat, wife of Abzu and mother of Enki, wanted revenge. She became a dragon and led an army of other monsters to destroy Enki and the gods. Only one god was brave enough to fight against Tiamat. He was Marduk, who shot an arrow into Tiamat's mouth that went straight to her heart.

Marduk cut Tiamat's body in two. He used one half to make the heavens and all its stars, and the other half to form the Earth. Her chest became the mountains, and from her eyes flowed the rivers Tigris and Euphrates. This is how the world began.

⬆ *Marduk aimed his arrow into the dragon Tiamat's mouth.*

MARDUK THE DRAGON-SLAYER

Marduk was the chief god of Babylon. Many myths were told about him. He was described as a hero who always defeated the forces of evil.

⬅ *Marduk (left, in a chariot) fights Tiamat.*

Once upon a time:
George and the dragon

LIBYA • • TURKEY

This myth comes from…

The city of Silene, in Libya, North Africa, was troubled by a dragon. At night, it breathed poison upon the people, who lived in fear of the monster.

The princess shook with fear at the sight of the mighty dragon.

Every day, the people took the dragon two sheep, and hoped it would leave them in peace. But there came a time when the townsfolk had used up nearly all their sheep, so they started to leave the dragon one sheep and one human.

The human victim was chosen at random, and one day the king's daughter was picked. At first, the king refused to let his daughter die, but he had no choice. Dressed in her wedding clothes, the princess was taken to the dragon's lair.

Life of St. George

St. George came from Cappadocia (part of modern-day Turkey) and lived in the AD 200s. He was a Christian, and he disagreed with the terrible way the Romans were treating the Christians. He was sent to prison by the Romans and killed for refusing to give up his Christian faith.

⬆ *George wounded the dragon with his spear, saving the princess's life.*

As the princess awaited her death, a traveler rode by. His name was George. The princess told him about the dragon, and he promised to save her. When the dragon came near, George rode towards it and wounded it with his spear. He told the princess to tie her belt around the dragon's neck and lead it into the city.

Saint day

On 23 April, people celebrate St. George's day. St. George is the **patron saint** of Aragon and Catalonia in Spain, as well as England, Georgia, Lithuania, Palestine, Portugal, Germany, and Greece.

On seeing the dragon, people fled in terror. George promised to kill the dragon on one condition—that the king and all his people became Christians. This they did, and so George slayed the monster and saved the townsfolk.

Dragons of China and Japan

The myths of China and Japan tell many stories about dragons. The dragons of China are usually described as friendly toward humans, but Japanese dragons can cause harm.

Both Chinese and Japanese dragons are wingless beasts with snaking, scaly bodies, four short legs, and sharp claws. Their heads are small and delicate, with whiskers and wispy beards. They have big ears, horns on their heads, and they breathe fire and smoke from their nostrils.

⬆ A white dragon and a blue dragon from the myths of China.

➡ Dragons are popular beasts in the folktales of China and Japan.

Dragon colors

Chinese dragons are very colorful. The colors have special meanings.
- A black dragon is in charge of lakes.
- A red dragon is in charge of rivers.
- A blue dragon is kind and brave.
- A yellow dragon can talk to the gods.
- A white dragon means a disaster will happen, such as a famine.

◄ *In a Chinese dragon dance, a team of dancers carries a colorful dragon made from cloth on poles above their heads.*

Dragon dance

The dragon dance is performed in China, at the start of the Chinese New Year. The dance began as a way to please the Chinese gods, in the hope they would give farmers a good year. Today, it is said to bring good luck.

The dragons' eyes are red, and inside their mouths they keep the "pearl of wisdom" (in China the pearl is a symbol of wisdom). They love jewelry, especially **jade**, and they avoid anything made from **iron** as this can hurt them.

21

Once upon a time: The dragon and the phoenix

• CHINA

This myth comes from...

A dragon and a phoenix (a mythical bird) lived on an island. One day, they found a beautiful pebble in the riverbed. They decided to polish the pebble until it became a round, white pearl.

When they were finished, they had created the most perfect treasure. The pearl gave off a soft, glowing light. As time passed, news of the precious pearl spread, until Xi Wangmu (say: *shee wang-moo*), the Queen Mother, learned about it. From this moment, she wanted it.

One night, as the dragon and the phoenix slept, the Queen Mother sent a servant to steal the jewel, and when he returned with the prize, she locked it away.

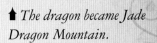

The dragon and the phoenix searched their island, but the pearl was nowhere to be found. It was only when they went to the Queen Mother's palace that they saw a familiar light—the light of the pearl.

⬆ The dragon became Jade Dragon Mountain.

⬅ The dragon and the phoenix discover who has taken their precious pearl.

Inside the palace, the Queen Mother was showing the pearl to her friends. Suddenly, the dragon and the phoenix rushed in to take back their treasure. In the struggle that followed, the pearl was thrown from a window. It hit the ground and became a lake. The dragon and the phoenix settled beside the lake. They became the mountains that still guard the treasure inside the lake from that day to this.

Once upon a time:
How the jellyfish lost its bones

• JAPAN

This myth comes from…

It is said that jellyfish used to have bones, fins, and feet. One day it lost them, and this is how it happened.

↓ King Ryujin was furious with Jellyfish for letting Monkey escape.

There was a Dragon King called Ryujin who lived in a wonderful palace at the bottom of the sea, built of red and white **coral**. Ryujin was a powerful dragon and it was he, and he alone, that controlled the tides. Turtles, fish, and jellyfish were all his servants.

One day, he ordered Jellyfish to bring Monkey to him, as Ryujin wanted to eat its liver. Jellyfish obeyed his master. When Jellyfish found Monkey, he explained that the Dragon King had asked to see him.

The pair began to swim to Ryujin's underwater palace. On the way, Jellyfish told Monkey what Ryujin planned to do. Monkey thought for a moment, then told Jellyfish that he had left his liver in a jar in the forest. He would gladly go back and collect it, and bring it to the Dragon King later. Jellyfish agreed, so he let Monkey go.

When Jellyfish told Ryujin that Monkey would be late coming to the palace, the Dragon King became angry. He could see that Monkey had tricked Jellyfish. In his rage, Ryujin hit Jellyfish so hard, its bones were crushed out of him—leaving a blob of boneless jelly.

Dragon Kings

Among the dragons of China and Japan are four described as Dragon Kings. These are the most powerful of all dragons, and each of them controls a different sea. In Japan, they are the Dragon King of the East Sea, South Sea, West Sea, and North Sea.

◄ Itsukushima **shrine**, Japan, where the daughter of Dragon King Ryujin is believed to live.

Dragon shrines

There are shrines (sacred places) in Japan linked with dragons. For example, Itsukushima shrine, on the island of Miyajima, is said to be where the daughter of Dragon King Ryujin lived.

Dragons of India

The ancient stories of India describe dragons and dragonlike creatures that existed at the very beginning of the world. Myths tell of great battles in which dragons are defeated.

As with Chinese and Japanese dragons, those of India are usually pictured as giant, wingless serpents. They have short legs, and some have many heads. Their long bodies are covered in scales. They breathe fire and smoke from their mouths and nostrils.

⬆ *Vritra, a three-headed dragon.*

➡ *Ananta, a serpent-dragon with many heads.*

Dragon hell

The dragons of India are said to live in an underground place known as Patala, which is a form of hell. It is where the souls of wicked humans are sent. They are guarded by dragons, and can never escape.

MOON-EATING DRAGON

According to an Indian myth, Rahu's dragon head was sliced off and thrown to the heavens, but it could not die. In revenge for being cut off, the head chases the Moon and eats it once a month. Sometimes it bites a chunk out of the Sun, which is when a **solar eclipse** happens—the Moon passes between the Sun and the Earth and blocks out the Sun's light.

◀ *Apalala, a serpent-dragon with two legs.*

▲ *When a solar eclipse took place, people believed the dragon Rahu had bitten a chunk out of the Sun.*

The most famous Indian serpent-dragon is Vritra, meaning "Encloser." A dragon with three heads, its vast body wrapped itself around the whole world. Another Indian dragon is Rahu, who has the body of a human and the head and tail of a dragon.

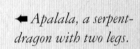

◀ *Rahu, a human-like monster with a dragon's head and tail.*

Once upon a time: The dragon and the sea

This myth comes from…

• INDIA

A priest called Tvashtri wanted his son Trisiras to become king of the gods. The true king was Indra, so when Indra saw that Trisiras was after his throne, he struck him dead.

Tvashtri was beside himself with grief over the death of his son, and he swore revenge against Indra. He created a huge serpent-dragon named Vritra. The serpent was so big it could reach into the heavens, and when Indra wasn't looking, Vritra stretched up and swallowed him.

Indra crawled out of Vritra's stomach and tickled its throat. The dragon spat him out. Indra now tried to fight Vritra, but the monster was always stronger.

➡ Indra used foam made by the sea to slay the dragon Vritra.

28

Indra asked the god Vishnu for advice. Vishnu told him to make peace with Vritra. The dragon agreed, but on condition that Indra never attacked it with any weapon made of wood, metal, or stone, with anything dry or wet, or during the day or night.

One day, Indra was by the sea. The sun was going down, so it was neither day nor night. A huge wave washed onto the shore, sending up a column of foam. Indra realized the foam wasn't wood, stone, or metal, and wasn't wet or dry. He seized the foam and brought it crashing down on Vritra, and the dragon was killed.

The rains come

In some versions of the Vritra myth, the serpent is said to have drunk all Earth's water, causing a terrible **drought**. But when Indra killed it, he released the trapped water from the serpent's body, causing the rain to fall.

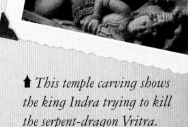

⬆ *This temple carving shows the king Indra trying to kill the serpent-dragon Vritra.*

GLOSSARY

Burial mound
A mound of soil raised up over a person's grave.

Coral
A hard red, pink, or white substance formed from the skeletons of tiny sea creatures. They grow beneath the sea, and are often found in groups that form a reef.

Cursed
When a curse has been put on a person, a place or an object, so that something bad or harmful happens.

Dragon-slayer
A person who slays (kills) a dragon.

Dragon-stone
A type of red stone thought to be formed from dragon's blood that has set hard.

Dragonship
A type of warship used by the Vikings, with a carved image of a dragon at the prow (front).

Drought
A long period of time without any rainfall.

Famine
A serious shortage of food that causes terrible hunger and even starvation.

Iron
A hard metal that is used to make steel.

Jade
A hard, green stone that can be carved to make jewelry and ornaments.

Lair
The place where an animal, particularly a dangerous one, lives.

Longship
A narrow warship used to transport Viking soldiers.

Middle Ages
A period of time in European history that starts around AD 450 and ends around AD 1500.

Patron saint
A saint who is seen as the special protector of a country or place.

Pendragon

A name given to warriors from Wales, UK, in the Middle Ages. It means "dragon head."

Phoenix

A mythical bird that is said to live for hundreds of years and then die in a fire. It then rises up from the ashes as a young bird, ready to live again.

Saint

A man or woman who leads a very holy life. Christians, as well as members of some other religions, worship saints.

Serpent

A very large snake. In stories and folktales, huge, terrifying snakes are often called serpents.

Shrine

A religious place where people to go to worship a particular god or person.

Solar eclipse

An event that happens when the Moon passes between the Sun and the Earth. The Sun is blocked out, making it appear dark, even in the middle of the day.

Standard

A type of flag carried into battle, or flown from a building.

Vikings

A group of people that came from Scandinavia, in the north of Europe. The Viking Age began about 1200 years ago and lasted for 300 years.

INDEX